HOW TO READ A COMIC BOOK

Comic books are made up of pictures in boxes, called panels. Look at each of these panels from left to right, and top to bottom.

Read the speech bubbles, caption boxes and any sound effects from left to right, too. Together with the images, these will tell you the story.

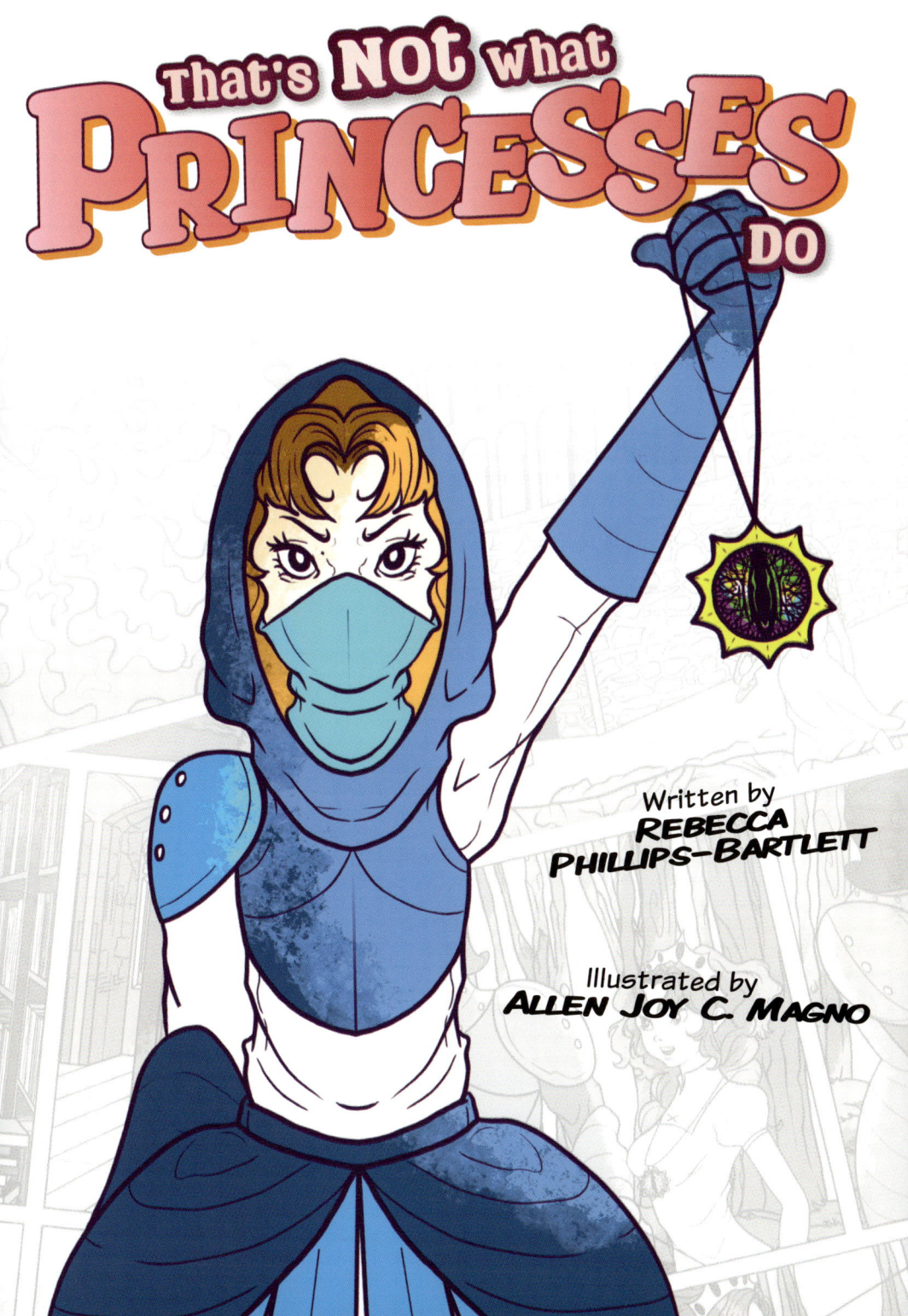

THUD!

ROAR!

... and it's angry.

We've got to stop it before it burns down the whole castle!

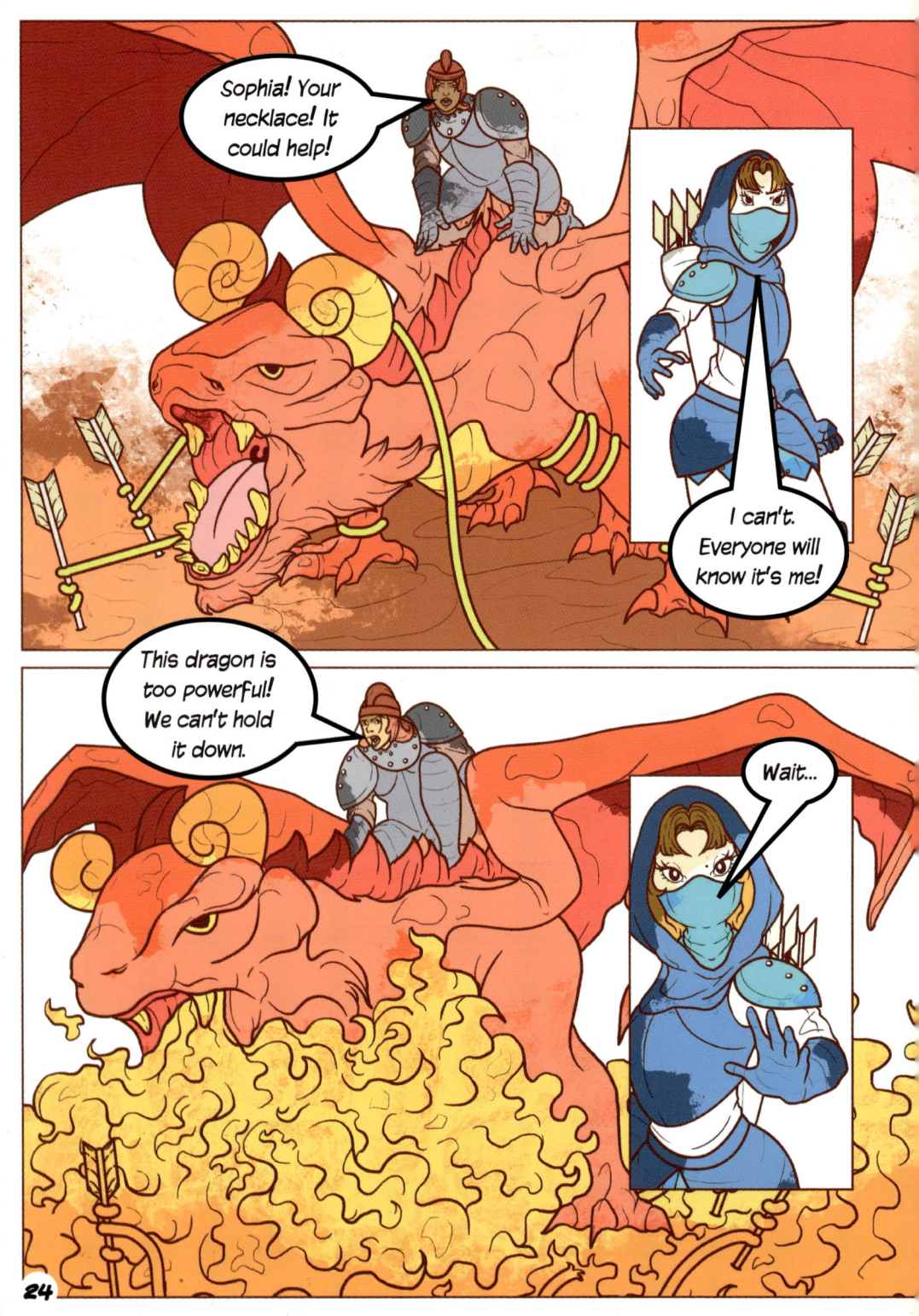

Silence fell on the battleground.

Where is the dragon?

Where did they go?

Look!

Sophia, have you learnt nothing from me? That is DEFINITELY NOT what princesses...

Shh... It's sleeping. Madame Grimmelda, there is clearly something special about this necklace...

Do not interu–

@2024 BookLife Publishing Ltd.
King's Lynn, Norfolk, PE30 4LS, UK

ISBN 978-1-80505-294-4

All rights reserved. Printed in India.
A catalogue record for this book is
available from the British Library.

That's Not What Princesses Do
Written by Rebecca Phillips-Bartlett
Illustrated by Allen Joy C. Magno

ABOUT BOOKLIFE GRAPHIC READERS

BookLife Graphic Readers are designed to encourage reluctant readers to take the next step in their reading adventure. These books are a perfect accompaniment to the BookLife Readers phonics scheme and are designed to be read by children who have a good grasp on reading but are reluctant to pick up a full-prose book. Graphic Readers combine graphic and prose storytelling in a way that aids comprehension and presents a more accessible reading experience for reluctant readers and lovers of comic books.

ABOUT THE AUTHOR

Rebecca loves storytelling. When she is not at work writing stories, she can often be found at the theatre teaching, performing or directing. Rebecca lives with her three cats who love to help her write by walking across the keyboard as she is typing.

ABOUT THE ILLUSTRATOR

Allen's artistic journey commenced at a young age, a perpetual exploration that has defined her life. From contributing to her high school's editorial newspaper to pursuing a Multimedia course at Mapua University, she cultivated her creative prowess. Intrigued by the publishing industry, Allen translated her passion into a career, delving into traditional printing and ebook creation at a Philippine publishing company post-graduation. Currently thriving as a graphic designer in a skills training company, she sustains her artistic pursuits. Allen envisions a lifelong commitment to art, fueled by the unwavering support of her family and friends, who serve as constant wellsprings of inspiration in her creative endeavors.